THE LISTENING CORNER STORYBOOK

Also available

LISTEN WITH MOTHER
MORE STORIES FROM LISTEN WITH MOTHER
ANIMAL TALES FROM LISTEN WITH MOTHER
NURSERY RHYMES AND SONGS FROM LISTEN WITH MOTHER

THE LISTENING CORNER STORYBOOK

With an introduction by
Irene Handl

Illustrated by Douglas Hall

*Published in association
with the BBC*

HUTCHINSON
London Melbourne Sydney Auckland Johannesburg

Hutchinson Children's Books Ltd
An imprint of the Hutchinson Publishing Group
17–21 Conway Street, London W1P 6JD

Hutchinson Publishing Group (Australia) Pty Ltd
16–22 Church Street, Hawthorn, Melbourne, Victoria 3122, Australia

Hutchinson Group (NZ) Ltd
32–24 View Road, PO Box 40-086, Glenfield, Auckland 10

Hutchinson Group (SA) Pty Ltd
PO Box 337, Bergvlei 2012, South Africa

First published 1985
Each story © the author 1985
Introduction © Irene Handl 1985
Illustrations © Douglas Hall 1985

Set in Baskerville by Book Ens, Saffron Walden, Essex

Printed and bound in Great Britain
by Anchor Brendon Ltd, Tiptree Essex

British Library Cataloguing in Publication Data

The Listening corner storybook.
1. Children's stories, English
I. Hall, Douglas, *1931–*
823'.01'089282[J]   PZ5

ISBN 0 09 159630 0

Contents

Introduction   7
 Irene Handl
The visitors   9
 Rachael Birley
Mr Sweet and Mr Sour   13
 Lee Pressman
Grandma buys a Bopper   17
 Janet Sorensen
Fox tricks   21
 Aidan Chambers
Mr Antonio   25
 David Willmott
Monty the monkey   28
 Lee Pressman
Sally and the magic rattle: the shore-people   32
 Joyce Dunbar
Grandad Gilbert the repairman   37
 Beryl Desmond
The pirate, the parrot and the peanuts   40
 Lee Pressman
Lion and Fox   43
 Aidan Chambers

The mice and the cat
Aidan Chambers
Sally and the magic rattle: surprise for King
Oldendays   46
Joyce Dunbar
Grandad Gilbert and the special car   55
Beryl Desmond
Mr Antonio's good turn   58
David Willmott
The fierce lion   62
Ann Ross
Grandma and Bopper Ball go to the
seaside   65
Janet Sorensen
Town Mouse and Country Mouse   69
Aidan Chambers
The crocodile with snappy jaws   73
Ann Ross
The Trimble Town Band   77
Beryl Desmond
Mrs Tippet's busy day   81
Valerie McCarthy
Bopper Ball goes out alone   84
Janet Sorensen
Acknowledgements

Introduction

Do you know, I never once 'Listened with Mother' as a child. Well, I couldn't could I? The programme first went on the air in the 50's, so *I* would have been around a cool 50, as well!

But though I missed out on 'Listen with Mother', I listened to my *own* mother, and how! *And* to my father, *and* to my older sister, *plus* to any grown-ups feeble enough to be pressed into service as Story-Reader to the Terrible Tyrant who was me. At an age when other infants were happily grappling with 'The Cat Sat on the Mat', I was steadfastly refusing all efforts to teach me to read. I was an *awful* kid.

Then the inevitable happened: Mutiny. Friend after friend stopped reading to me, unable to utter another syllable. At first I couldn't believe it. I simply refused to accept the fact that from then on no one was ever going to read to me again. But there it was. And lucky for me, because it was in that Terrible Silence that I actually began to teach myself to read.

And now we have *The Listening Corner*, am I glad that I sat with that Cat on that Mat. 'Cause who's in *The Listening Corner* today? It's me! Irene Handl (or Grandma and the Bopper if you'd rather) discovering all these wonderful children's stories *for myself,* and loving every minute of it!

Irene Handl

The visitors
Rachael Birley

There was once a little girl who said to her mother, 'I'd like to have someone to tea.'

Her mother said, 'Who would you like to have to tea, the butcher, the baker or the candlestick maker?'

The little girl said, 'I don't want to have any of those people to tea.' She thought hard, and then she said, 'I want to have the Nimbleby of Fisk to tea.'

'The Nimbleby of Fisk,' said her mother, 'what is he like, I don't think I've met him.'

'He's very nice,' said the little girl. 'He's quite fat and he wears gold clothes.'

'All right,' said her mother, 'I'll ring him,' and she went to the telephone.

'He can come,' she said, when she had finished telephoning, 'and he will be here at three. What do you think he likes to eat?'

'Smartie sandwiches,' said the little girl.

At three o'clock precisely the doorbell rang, and there was the Nimbleby of Fisk himself, very grandly dressed, with a green and gold cloak and a pink and gold hat. They ate smartie sandwiches and played with the train set until it was time for him to go.

The next day, the little girl said to her mother, 'I'd like to have somebody to tea.'

Her mother said, 'Who would you like to have to tea, the Man in the Moon?'

The little girl said, 'I don't want to have him to tea, he only likes cold porridge. I want to have the Dremingham Snork.'

'What is the Dremingham Snork like?' asked her mother.

'She is tall and rather bossy, and her hair is green,' said the little girl, 'but I like her.'

'All right,' said her mother, 'I'll see if she can come.' And she went to the telephone.

'The Dremingham Snork says that she would be *delighted*, and will be here *promptly* at half past three.'

'What does the Dremingham Snork eat?' asked the mother. 'I hope it's not anything too difficult; I haven't got much time to make anything.'

'She isn't difficult,' said the little girl. 'She eats chocolate biscuit sandwiches with jam in the middle. Red jam.'

'How lucky. I haven't got any black or orange jam, but I have got red jam,' said her mother.

Punctually at half past three, the doorbell rang. The Dremingham Snork was wearing her best gold velvet pantaloons, with an orange satin coat and a tall Snorkely hat made of sunflower seeds. She ate nearly all the chocolate biscuit sandwiches and only left one for the little girl. But she was very good at playing families, and let the little girl be Baby nearly all the time. So the little girl was quite sorry when it was time for the Dremingham Snork to go.

The next day, the little girl said to her mother, 'I want to have someone to tea.'

'Who would you like this time,' said her mother, 'Humpy Dumpty?'

'No,' said the little girl. 'He might get broken. I want to have Janey who lives round the corner.'

'All right,' said her mother, 'I'll ring up and see if she can come.' When she put the phone down, she said, 'Janey's Mum says Janey can come and she will bring her round at four o'clock.'

'What does Janey eat?' asked the little girl's mother.

'She eats almost anything,' said the little girl, 'but mostly peanut butter sandwiches.'

'Smooth or crunchy?' said the mother.

'Crunchy is her best,' said the little girl.

Just as the clock struck four, the doorbell rang and there was Janey who lived round the corner. She was wearing a long red skirt that belonged to her big sister, a blue table-cloth for a train and a beautiful silver crown with coloured jewels.

'I am the Queen,' said Janey. 'You can be King if you like.'

'All right,' said the little girl, 'because I *am* wearing trousers.'

They played at kings and queens all through tea, and after tea they played at houses. Janey did the cooking and the little girl did the shopping. Janey didn't want to go home at all, when her mum came to fetch her.

'You *have* had a lot of people to tea this week,' said the mother to the little girl as she climbed into bed that night.

'Yes,' said the little girl. 'But I think I liked Janey best.'

Mr Sweet and Mr Sour

Lee Pressman

There was once a King and he had two cooks. One cook was called Sid Sweet and he loved to make food for the King that tasted sugary and sweet – like treacle pudding, toffees and iced cakes.

The other cook was called Stan Sour and he liked to make the King food that tasted sharp and sour – like vinegar dressing, sour cream dips and lemon drops.

The King liked his two cooks and he liked all the food they made but the problem was that the two cooks didn't like one another.

'All the food that you make for the King is too sugary and sweet,' said Stan Sour. 'It can't be good for his teeth.'

'Rubbish,' replied Sid Sweet. 'All the sour food that you make can't be good for the King's stomach.'

'You don't know what you're talking about,' snapped Stan Sour.

'And *you* don't know what *you're* talking about,' shouted Sid Sweet. 'Everybody knows that sweet food is best.'

'No, sour food is best.'

'Sweet.'

'Sour.'

'Sweet.'

'Sour.'

'Oh do stop it, you two,' ordered the King. 'I can't stand all this arguing and bickering any longer. You don't understand, sometimes I like sweet food and other times I like sour food. If you two can't get on together, I'll have to get rid of you both. There are other cooks in the Kingdom you know. Like Sam Salt and Steve Spice; they're both supposed to be very good. Now I'll give you one more chance. Go off to the kitchen and work together. I want you to make something really tasty for my tea, something that I can eat either sweet or sour depending on how I feel at the time.'

The two cooks looked at each other quite bewildered. Sid Sweet scratched his head. Stan Sour kicked his heels. They'd never worked together before and they'd certainly never made anything that could be eaten sweet or sour.

They wandered back to the kitchen in a daze, wondering what they could make the King for tea.

'How about a sour treacle pudding?' suggested Sid Sweet. 'No, that doesn't sound very nice.'

'What about some vinegar-flavoured chocolate cake?' said Stan Sour. 'No, perhaps not.'

They thought and thought and looked through their recipe books but couldn't seem to come up with what they were looking for.

'It'll soon be tea-time,' said Sid Sweet. 'If we don't think of something soon, we're going to lose our jobs.'

Stan Sour still had his nose buried in one of the cookery books and was reading out loud all the dishes.

'Pease pudding, porridge, popadoms, pineapple pudding, pancakes—'

'Wait a moment,' interrupted Sid Sweet. 'What did you just say?'

'Pineapple pudding,' answered Stan Sour.

'No, after that.'

'Er . . . pancakes.'

'That's it,' screamed Sid Sweet, throwing his

hat up into the air with delight. 'That's what we'll make for the King. Pancakes.'

'Of course,' laughed Stan Sour. 'What a brilliant idea. We'll make the King a whole pile of pancakes and he can eat them either with lemon juice if he wants them sour or with treacle or jam if he wants them sweet. Come on, Sid, let's get busy with the batter.'

So, laughing and chatting and singing, the two cooks began to make pancakes. They cracked the eggs, mixed the batter, tossed the pancakes and at tea-time carried to the King's table a big plate of pancakes.

'Excellent,' said the King. 'I'll squeeze some lemon juice on my first pancake. Hmmmm. That tastes sharp but very tasty. Now I'll have jam on my next one. Mmmm. That's sweet and also very nice. Now I think I'll have lemon juice and sugar on my next pancake . . . sweet and sour. Hmmmm. Absolutely delicious. Well done, you two. Good work.'

Sid Sweet and Stan Sour were so pleased with their success and were so happy to be friends that from then on they always worked together and came up with some really fine food for the King.

'What have you made for my supper tonight, boys? Oh, my favourite . . . sweet and sour pork. Scrumptious!'

Grandma buys a Bopper

Janet Sorensen

Grandma lived alone all by herself in a tiny flat with a tiny garden and an old garden shed.

Grandma had two little granddaughters who lived a long way away, but she was always looking into toy shops for 'something for the girls'.

'Just in *case* I can go and see them. I wish it wasn't so far to go to see the girls,' said Grandma, looking out of the window. 'A taxi is too expensive, and I'm too old and stiff to ride a bicycle. Don't like trains and the buses. Well, you have to wait so long, and I have to get three different buses.'

Grandma put her coat on and went out shopping. On her way home she passed the toy shop, and looked in the window, 'just in case there's something for the girls'.

Sitting in the middle of the window was a *huge* rubber ball, a reddy orange colour with two long wriggly ears at the top. A notice read, 'Go a long way on a Space Bopper!'

'Oooh!' said Grandma. 'I'd like to go a long way . . . to see the girls.'

Grandma went into the shop.

'Good morning,' she said to the shopkeeper. 'I'd like one of those Bopper things please . . . for the girls.'

When she had paid for it and had come out of the shop, she looked at the box.

'Doesn't look the same shape as the one in the window,' said Grandma. 'Can't go *anywhere* on *that*!'

When she got home she undid the box and there was a piece of paper which said 'How to blow up the Bopper'.

'Oooh,' said Grandma. 'I've got to blow it up.'

Grandma found the mouthpiece place and started to blow. Grandma's face got redder and redder but the *flat* shape stayed . . . flat.

'Whew!' said Grandma. 'I know, I'll take it to the garage where they pump up tyres.'

The man at the garage smiled at Grandma... and started to blow up the Bopper with the tyre pump, which he fixed to the hole in the Bopper's side. When he had finished, the Bopper was very big and round... *and* hard to carry. Grandma peeped round the corner of the garage.

'No one looking,' said Grandma, and climbed on the Bopper.

Bounce... bounce... bounce... went the Bopper. Grandma held on tight. The Bopper bounced along and the bounces got bigger and bigger. BOUNCE... BOUNCE... BOUNCE.

'Oooooh!' said Grandma. 'This is lovely.'

Suddenly, Bopper gave a very big bounce, and started to go up, up, up, into the sky... *and didn't come down.*

'Whee, whee. I like this!' said Grandma. 'I like this very much.'

Everything down below looked so small. Grandma began to enjoy floating along so high up – but she held on very tightly to the Bopper's ears.

'Wheee, wheee,' said the Bopper. He was feeling very happy, as they floated past aeroplanes and helicopters.

Then Grandma shouted out, 'The girls! The

girls!' And far down below in a garden were her two little granddaughters.

'Let's go down,' said Grandma. 'I want to see the girls.' And so the Bopper floated gently down . . . and landed in the garden.

'You've come! You've come!' shouted the girls.

'Yes,' said Grandma, puffing, 'and my magic Bopper!'

'Bounce, bounce, bounce,' said the Bopper. Grandma showed him to her granddaughters, and let them bounce along too – but they didn't go right up into the sky. That was only for Grandma.

Fox tricks

Aidan Chambers

One morning Fox set out to find food for her family. She had a lot of children and they were very hungry. So Fox ran fast. But she didn't look where she was going. She didn't notice the fallen branch and she didn't notice the deep pond. She tripped over the branch and fell ... *splash* ... into the pond.

Fox struggled and kicked and shouted, 'Help! Help!' but it was no use. She couldn't get out and no one was near who could help. All she could do was paddle about in the water and hope that someone would come along soon.

After a while Goat came clambering along the edge of the pond. He heard Fox splashing about in the water. 'Hello, Fox,' Goat said, 'What are you doing in there?'

Now Fox liked playing tricks on her friends, even when she was in trouble. 'What do you think I'm doing?' she said. 'I'm having a drink, of course.'

It was a very hot day. Goat's tongue was hanging out. 'Is the water good?' he asked.

'Delicious,' Fox said, lapping up another mouthful. 'It's sweet and soft and cool.'

'I'm very thirsty too,' Goat said, licking his lips.

'Come and join me,' Fox said. 'There's plenty of room.'

Without thinking any more about it, Goat jumped into the pond.

Then, Fox scrambled on to Goat's back, and climbed on to his head, and then jumped up, out of the pond, on to the bank.

'Thank you, Goat,' she shouted. 'I needed your help to get out of there.'

'But what about me?' Goat cried. 'The water is deeper than I thought. How can I get out?'

'I don't know,' Fox said. 'But always remember: Look before you leap.'

And Fox ran off, laughing, and left Goat spluttering in the pond.

Later that day Fox saw the farmyard Cock sitting on a fence, sunning himself. 'What a tasty meal Cock would be,' Fox thought. So she hid behind a bush and waited for her chance.

'What a beautiful bird I am,' Cock clucked to himself. He smoothed his feathers and stuck out his chest. Then he crowed loudly to tell the world, and all his hens, how wonderful he was.

Fox came from behind the bush and trotted up to the fence. 'Good morning, Cock,' she said. 'You *are* singing well today.'

'Thank you,' said Cock. 'I do have a fine voice, even if I say so myself.'

'You do, you do!' Fox said. 'Will you sing something just for me?'

'I would be glad to,' Cock said, and he closed his eyes and threw back his head, and crowed loudly again.

Fox saw her chance. She sprang up, grabbed Cock by the throat, and ran off. Cock screamed and struggled. 'Put me down!' he squawked. 'Help! Help!'

The farmer heard Cock and saw what was happening. 'Stop, thief!' he cried and chased after Fox who was running towards the wood with Cock flapping in her mouth.

All the other farm animals heard the farmer shout and they followed him, chasing after Fox. The pigs, the cows, the geese, the sheep, the horses, the dogs, and, of course, all of Cock's many hens.

'They're after you,' Cock shouted to Fox. But Fox ran on. She knew she could run faster than any farm animal.

Cock knew that too.

'Oh, Fox,' Cock cried. 'What an amazing runner you are. They'll never catch you. You should tell them so.'

Fox felt pleased. She turned her head and shouted: 'You're too slow. This bird's mine!'

But as soon as Fox opened her mouth, Cock flapped his wings and flew up into a tree.

Fox dared not stop or she'd be caught. She ran on, into the wood.

'What a fool I am,' she said to herself. 'Sometimes it's better to keep your mouth shut.' And so Fox's family went hungry that day, and Fox learned that if you play tricks on others, you shouldn't be surprised if they play tricks on you.

Mr Antonio

David Willmott

Mr Antonio was small and dark with a nice wiggly moustache, and he didn't just sell ice cream – he *made* it. It was soft and creamy and he had learned how to make it from his mother.

Mr Antonio and his mother came from a country called Italy, where they make a lot of ice cream. It's the place where the very first ice cream was made.

Mr Antonio made strawberry ice cream, vanilla ice cream, chocolate ice cream and pistachio – that's the one with the nuts inside.

He put his ice cream into little plastic boxes, and then he put the plastic boxes inside a big plastic box. After that he put the big plastic box inside a big wooden box on the front of his tricycle. Then, he would ride along the road, ringing his bell, and shouting, 'Ice-a-creama . . . ice-a-creama.'

Every day Mr Antonio would cycle along a straight road with tall trees on each side, up a hill, down the other side, and over a little bridge to the village where the children lived.

When he arrived Mr Antonio rang his bell, and all the children came running out of their houses to buy an ice cream.

'You tell me what you want,' said Mr Antonio. 'I gotta strawberry ice-a-creama, vanilla ice-a-creama, chocolate ice-a-creama, and pistachio – that's the one with the nuts inside.'

One morning, it was raining, but Mr Antonio made his ice cream, put it into little plastic boxes and those little plastic boxes were put inside a big plastic box. After that the big plastic box was put inside the big wooden box on the front of Mr Antonio's tricycle.

Mr Antonio cycled along the straight road with tall trees on each side, up the hill and then, oh dear, the road was wet, and down the hill he went – faster, and faster. The tricycle started to slide and slide, then fell over. It rolled over and over until it stopped at the bottom of the hill.

Poor Mr Antonio got up, brushed the mud off his trousers, and put his tricycle back on its wheels. He rang his bell and it still worked, but when he looked inside the ice-cream box, the lids had fallen off the little plastic boxes and all the ice cream was mixed up.

Poor Mr Antonio felt very unhappy as he pushed his tricycle along the road, over the bridge and into the village. He didn't ring his bell, but the children still came running out to buy their ice cream.

'Hello,' said Mr Antonio. 'I'm sorry, but my tricycle fell over and all the ice cream is mixed up together,' and he lifted the lid of the ice cream box to show them.

'That's all right,' said one little boy, 'I like things all mixed up. It's like the trifle my mum makes. I'll call it *trifle* ice cream.'

Now, when Mr Antonio rings his bell and the children come running out, he says, 'I gotta strawberry ice-a-creama, vanilla ice-a-creama, chocolate ice-a-creama, pistachio – that's the one with the nuts, and I got *TRIFLE* ice-a-creama.'

He makes it specially, all the flavours mixed up together, because the children like it so much.

Monty the monkey

Lee Pressman

It was Monday morning and Monty the Monkey was starting his new job. His Uncle Max owned the grocery shop where all the animals bought their food. Uncle Max wanted Monty to go round on his bike and deliver some of the groceries to the animals' houses.

Uncle Max started to give Monty the food, and the young monkey packed it into the little basket on his bike.

'I want you to take this carrot to Parrot, and here's a marrow for Sparrow, and some mousse for Goose. Have you got that, lad?' said Uncle Max, handing Monty the jar.

'Oh yes, Uncle, I'll remember that,' answered Monty.

'Also,' continued the old monkey, 'here's some tea for Bee, a cake for Drake who lives on the lake, and some pears for the three Bears who live upstairs. That's all for now. Off you go lad.'

The basket on Monty's bike was now piled high with all the food for the animals. He climbed on to the saddle and pedalled off down the lane.

Soon he came to Parrot's house. He stopped the bike. 'Now what food was I supposed to give Parrot?' he thought. 'Let me try to remember what Uncle told me . . . um . . . a marrow for Goose, some mousse for Bee, a carrot for the cake . . . no, that can't be right . . . er some pears for the stairs? Oh dear, I'm in such a muddle!'

Just then, Parrot stuck his head out of the window. 'Come on, Monty Monkey, haven't you got anything for me?'

Monty looked into the basket and gave Parrot the cake by mistake. Then he rode off quickly to Sparrow's house where Mrs Sparrow was waiting outside.

'If only I wasn't so muddled and could remember what to give her,' thought Monty.

'Let me think... some tea for the three Bears, a lake for the carrot, a Drake for the marrow who lives up the pears ... oh dear, that doesn't sound right, does it?'

Monty gave Mrs Sparrow the carrot and rode away quickly before she could say a word. He was so muddled that he just couldn't remember who to give what, and all the animals that Monday morning got the wrong food.

When Monty arrived back at the shop with an empty basket, Uncle Max was waiting by the door.

'How did you get on, lad?' he asked.

Monty blushed and looked down at his feet. 'Well actually, I did get a tiny bit muddled,' he said.

Just at that moment there was a terrible commotion, as into the shop burst ... Parrot, Sparrow, Goose, Bee, Drake, and the three Bears ... They were all clutching the wrong food that Monty had given them and were shouting loudly.

'I asked for a carrot and I got a cake,' screeched Parrot. 'I hate cakes!'

'I wanted some tea and I got this huge marrow,' buzzed Bee.

'All right, all right,' said Uncle Max. 'We'll sort it out.'

He explained to the angry animals that it was

Monty's first day at the job and he had got a bit muddled and was truly sorry.

'Tomorrow I'll get him to write out a list – that will help him remember,' said Uncle Max. 'As for now,' he continued, 'I've got a wonderful idea. Why don't we all take the food we've got outside the shop and have a picnic together as it's such a lovely sunny day.'

All the animals cheered. As they sat enjoying their suprise picnic they all agreed that if it hadn't been for Monty getting all their food so muddled, they wouldn't have been sitting there in the sun having such fun. Not a bad first day's work for muddled Monty Monkey.

Sally and the magic rattle: the shore-people

Joyce Dunbar

Do you have a favourite place to hide? Sally does. In her parents' bedroom, between two wardrobes, is a big mirror with a shelf, and underneath the shelf hangs a curtain pulled across to make a little cupboard for shoes and slippers. That's where Sally goes to be on her own, to think and dream.

Sally has a secret too. She has a magic rattle. It was given to her as a farewell present by an old lady who used to live in the same block of flats. Sally had been watching the removal van from her balcony three floors up, waiting to wave goodbye, when the old lady had called to her.

She had presented Sally with an old silver rattle. 'For me?' asked Sally, thinking it must be meant for Tim, her baby brother.

'For you,' answered the old lady. 'It's a magic rattle. You must close your eyes, shake the rattle and say these words:

> Rattle me, rattle me,
> Roll me round.
> Close your eyes,
> Hear my sound.
> Let me take you
> Where I will,
> Under the ground,
> Over the hill.

Sally thanked the old lady very much and ran off with the rattle – to her cupboard of course, where she wouldn't be disturbed. Making a little space for herself amongst the shoes, she closed her eyes, repeated the words and gently shook the rattle.

What did she hear? It was the sound of the sea! She opened her eyes and blinked in surprise.

For Sally was no longer in the dark bedroom cupboard but dazzled by sunlight on a lovely sandy shore. In her hand was the magic rattle; beside her a bucket and spade.

She got to work straight away building a sandcastle. She built turrets and a courtyard and a moat with a bridge. Then she paddled barefoot by the water's edge collecting seaweed and shells to decorate the castle. It was the best she'd ever made. She had just put in a seashell for the door when it opened wide!

'Come in, come in,' said a little voice. 'Tea is on the table.'

A crab stood holding the door. 'Come on in,' he said again. 'The shore-people are waiting.'

'Who are they?' asked Sally.

'The people who live on the sea-shore, of course,' replied the crab.

Sally walked through the door of the castle she had built, which had grown mysteriously bigger (or perhaps she had grown much smaller) and found herself in a banqueting hall with shell-shaped windows and seaweed drapes. There sat shore-lords and shore-ladies, round a table of mother-of-pearl. A place was laid specially for Sally.

'Have some seaweed soup,' said a shore-lord.

'And some jelly-fish jelly,' said a shore-lady.

'And a sand sandwich,' said a shrimp who waited on them.

Sally was just about to taste the jelly-fish jelly when everyone jumped up from the table. 'Run!' shouted a shore-lord. 'The tide's coming in!'

Sure enough, through the door and all the windows, the sea was flooding the castle. Sally ran with the shore-people across the bridge, over the moat, away from the incoming tide.

The shore-people looked sad. Some were weeping quietly. 'This is always happening,' they said. 'No sooner do we settle down in a nice new castle than the tide drives us out. If only you children would build them further inland.'

'That was the best we ever had.'

'Never mind,' said Sally. 'I'll build you a better one, here, away from the tide.'

And so she did. The shore-people were so pleased. 'You must be our guest of honour,' they said to Sally, and dressed her in a turquoise gown. Shells were sounded like trumpets and Sally shook her rattle as she led the way through the door of the new castle . . . straight into her parents' bedroom.

'Where have you been, Sally?' said her mother. 'I've been looking everywhere for you. And what are you doing in my turquoise dress? Take it off and go and play with Tim while I get tea ready.'

In the furthest corner of the cupboard, Sally hid the magic rattle. 'Look, Tim,' she said to her brother, 'I've brought you a seashell . . .'

Grandad Gilbert the repairman
Beryl Desmond

Ben loved having a grandad who owned a garage. 'My grandad can mend everything,' he told his friends.

It was true. Grandad Gilbert always had lots of interesting things to mend.

One day Ben and his grandad were eating their sandwiches, when Miss Todd drove into the garage 'Hello,' she called. 'I wonder if you can help me?'

Grandad got up. 'Having trouble with your car, Miss Todd?' he asked.

'No,' she said, 'my sewing machine has broken down. Everyone in the village says you're good at repairing things so can you mend my sewing machine?'

She opened the car boot and Grandad lifted out the sewing machine.

'My grandad is a good mender,' Ben told Miss Todd.

Grandad smiled, 'I'll have a look at it for you,' he promised. 'I expect you'll miss not being able to use your sewing machine.

'I don't like sewing really,' said Miss Todd. 'I'd much rather be out of doors gardening, but I've promised to make three bridesmaids' dresses.'

Ben helped his grandad carry the machine into the workshop. 'I'll let you know when I've fixed it,' he promised.

'Thank you,' said Miss Todd, and she drove away.

'She really misses her garden since she moved to her tiny flat,' Grandad sighed.

After lunch, Ben was watching his grandad working when another visitor arrived. It was Miss Box. 'Hello,' she said. 'My lawnmower's not working. Do you think you could mend it for me, please?'

Ben smiled. 'My grandad will be able to repair it,' he said.

'I'll certainly look at it for you,' said Grandad,

carrying the mower into the garage. 'You'll be needing it to cut your lawns.'

Miss Box sighed. 'Yes, and I don't really like gardening. I'd much rather be indoors, sewing,' and she went away.

As he watched Grandad working, Ben was thinking. 'Grandad, if Miss Box likes sewing why can't she make the bridesmaids' dresses for Miss Todd,' he said. 'I'm sure Miss Todd would like working in Miss Box's garden. They could swop.'

Grandad Gilbert thought Ben's idea was very clever.

The next morning when the two ladies called at the garage they were very pleased to find their machines mended. However, they were even more pleased when they heard Ben's idea.

'I'd love to sew the bridesmaids' dresses,' said Miss Box as she collected her lawnmower.

'And I'd love to take care of your garden,' said Miss Todd, as she collected her sewing machine.

Watching them leave, Grandad smiled. 'There go two satisfied customers,' he said.

Then, locking up the garage, he and Ben set off home for tea.

The pirate, the parrot and the peanuts

Lee Pressman

There was once a pirate who had a parrot, and this parrot liked to sit on the pirate's shoulder. But this particular parrot had a very annoying habit. It was always cracking peanuts in the pirate's ear – this used to make the pirate very angry.

'Stop cracking those noisy nuts in my ear,' cried the pirate. 'It's making me go quite deaf.' But the parrot loved his peanuts so much that he just couldn't stop.

'Oh my poor ears,' moaned the pirate. 'I can't stand this no more.'

He took the parrot down from his shoulder and put the bird in a cage.

'Now I'll get myself a new pet to sit on my shoulder,' said the pirate. 'A pet that doesn't make such a noise with its food.'

So the pirate went out and bought a cat. But that was no good because the cat used to sit on his shoulder eating fish and the smell of the fish used to drive the pirate mad. So he got rid of the cat and bought a monkey. But the monkey used to sit on his shoulder and eat bananas. Then he would throw the banana skins on the floor and the pirate would step on them and slip over. And this of course used to drive the pirate mad and he had to get rid of the monkey.

'If only my poor old parrot wouldn't crack those noisy nuts in my ear, I could have her sitting back on my shoulder,' said the pirate.

And then he had a wonderful idea. He rushed off to the market and came back later carrying a large barrel. On the side of the barrel were the words PEANUT BUTTER. The pirate took the barrel down to his cabin where the parrot was sitting sadly in her cage.

'Try some of this, me hearty,' laughed the pirate, handing the parrot a peanut butter sandwich. The parrot nibbled it in silence then squawked: 'Tastes just like peanuts.'

'It's better than peanuts, it's peanut butter,' said the pirate. 'Now you can come out of your cage and sit back on my shoulder and eat peanut butter sandwiches to your heart's content and I'll have no more cracking in my ear.'

So the happy bird climbed back on to the pirate's shoulder and there she stayed for many a long year ... the pirate, the parrot and the peanut butter sandwiches.

Lion and Fox

Aidan Chambers

One day Lion was ill. He must have been very ill because he roared and moaned and whimpered and sighed. And he didn't leave his cave, but lay at the door, waiting for someone to come and visit him.

No one did, of course. Everyone was afraid of Lion because if he caught you, he ate you. But after a while a little sparrow who was very nosey flew down and pecked around just out of reach of Lion's huge paw. And when Lion didn't move, or try to catch him, the little sparrow said,

'Good morning, Lion. Aren't you well?'

'No,' Lion said. 'I'm not. I'm right poorly.'

Sparrow gave Lion a good looking over, then flew off to tell the other animals what he'd seen.

'Lion really is ill,' Sparrow told the others. 'He's just lying there at the door of his cave making terrible noises.'

'We'll go and visit him,' the other animals said. 'After all, he is our King, and if he really is ill he won't eat us or hurt us, will he?'

The first animal to visit Lion was Goat, who took Lion a present of nice fresh berries to eat. Then Donkey wandered along, taking some of the best hay he could find. Crow visited too, taking some ripe cheese, and a family of mice paid a call.

The strange thing was that none of them was seen afterwards. 'Where's Goat?' asked some of Goat's friends next day. 'And where's Donkey? And what about Crow, and the mice?'

Fox said, 'I'll go and visit Lion. I'll find out what happened to Goat and Donkey and Crow and the mice.' So he trotted away and came to Lion's cave. But he didn't go inside. He didn't even go near enough for Lion to run out and catch him. He could see, though, that Lion was still there, lying in the doorway of his cave, moaning quietly to himself and looking sick.

'Morning, Lion,' Fox said, cheerfully.

'Hello, Fox,' Lion said sorrowfully, 'Why haven't you been to see me sooner?'

Fox said: 'I've just heard the news. How are you feeling today?'

Lion said: 'A little better, thank you. Won't you come inside and have a chat?'

Fox shook his head. 'Not today, thank you,' he said.

Lion said, 'Why not? I'm too weak to do anything but talk.'

'Is that right?' Fox said, grinning. 'I don't think Goat and Donkey and Crow and the mice would agree.'

'What do you mean?' Lion said.

Fox said, 'They all visited you, didn't they?'

'They did,' Lion said.

'I know,' Fox said. 'I can see their paw marks in the sand outside your cave. All the marks are going into your cave. But I can't see any of them coming out. So if you don't mind, Lion, I'll just trot off and see about my dinner.'

And Fox ran off, chuckling to himself: 'Lion thought he was cunning, but he isn't as cunning as me.' And all the other animals laughed when they heard what Fox had done.

The mice and the cat

Aidan Chambers

One day, all the mice held a meeting to talk about Cat. They were very frightened because Cat gave them no peace. She never stopped prowling about looking for mice to eat.

'Cat's so quiet,' one of the mice said, 'that I never hear her coming.'

'And she keeps herself so clean,' another mouse said, 'I never smell her coming either.'

'And she moves so fast,' they all agreed, 'that we can never escape. She plays with us, and throws us into the air, and catches us with her sharp claws and then eats us.' They shivered as they thought of the cruel things Cat did.

'We could always move house,' a very young mouse said.

'No, no!' a very old mouse said. 'My family came here in my grandfather's time. I'm not moving out just because of Cat.'

They all sat in silence again, listening to the old clock ticking, and the sound of people's footsteps on the floor above their heads. And they thought and thought.

Then the very young mouse jumped up and shouted: 'I know, I know, I know: let's put something really nasty in Cat's milk. That might frighten her off. Or,' he went on, even more excited, 'we could all rush at Cat at the same time and tickle her to death!'

'Quiet! Be quiet!' ordered the old mouse. 'Can't you understand: Cat is cruel and dangerous and cunning. She lies in wait for us, and then pounces, suddenly, fast enough to take your breath away. If you can't be serious, go somewhere else and play.'

The young mouse almost burst into tears. 'I am being serious,' he said. He'd only been trying to make useful suggestions.

But before he could begin to cry another idea came into his head. 'Could I say something else, please?' he said as politely as he knew how. 'If it's sensible,' the old mouse said.

The very young mouse took a deep breath and spoke very clearly and slowly to show how serious he was. 'The trouble is, we can't hear when Cat is coming. Is that right?'

'Yes, yes,' said the old mouse.

'But if we could hear her coming, we could run away before she reaches us?'

'Yes, yes,' the old mouse said. 'We all know that. Get on with it.'

'Well,' the young mouse said very seriously, 'Why don't we tie a little bell round Cat's neck. Then, every time she moves the bell would ring, and we would always know where she was and hear her coming.'

There was a silence while all the mice thought about this. And soon they began to nod. 'Of course!' they said. 'Of course! What a brilliant idea! And what a clever young mouse you are!' There were loud squeaks of praise, and the clapping of paws, and the thumping of tails on the floor. They patted the young mouse on the back, and gave him special mouthfuls of cheese as a reward.

The very young mouse smiled with pleasure and stuck out his chest with pride. Now they would be safe from Cat and everyone was happy. Everyone except the very old mouse. He sat stroking his old white whiskers, his face still as serious as before.

When the noise of cheering and excitement had died down, he looked at the other mice and said, 'Now just wait a minute.'

'What is it?' they all shouted.

'I have a question,' the old mouse said. 'My question is this: Which one of you is brave enough to climb on Cat's back and hang the bell round her neck?'

There was another silence. 'Oh dear,' the very young mouse said at last. 'I didn't think of that!'

'No, nor did the rest of you,' the old mouse said. 'So remember: Before deciding on a plan, always be sure you can do it.'

And from that day to this, no mouse has ever been able to think of a way of getting rid of Cat.

Sally and the magic rattle: a surprise for King Oldendays

Joyce Dunbar

Sally was very excited. It was her friend's birthday and she'd been invited to the party in a flat two floors down.

'Is it time to go yet?' she asked.

'No,' answered Sally's mother. 'There's an hour to wait.'

'How long is an hour?' asked Sally.

'Long enough for you to play one more game,' said her mother.

'Or to have one more adventure,' thought

Sally. The magic rattle was just where she'd left it, in the curtained cupboard in her parents' bedroom. Making herself comfortable she repeated the magic rhyme:

> Rattle me, rattle me,
> Roll me round.
> Close your eyes,
> Hear my sound.
> Let me take you
> Where I will,
> Under the ground,
> Over the hill.

Then . . . she heard . . . a bell ringing . . . and a murmuring of voices. She opened her eyes to find herself amongst a crowd of people in a castle courtyard.

'Oyez! Oyez! Oyez!' cried the bell-ringer.

'Where am I?' she asked a little boy.

'Oldendays Castle, of course,' said the boy. 'Look! Here comes King Oldendays on to the balcony!'

The crowd began to cheer. King Oldendays waved. He wore an Oldendays crown and an Oldendays cloak, but he did look very fed up.

'What day is it tomorrow?' he asked the people.

'YOUR BIRTHDAY!' they all shouted.

'And what will I get on my birthday?' asked the king.

'A silver bow with golden arrows,' said a man.

'A new jewel for your crown,' said a woman.

'A sugar mouse,' said a child.

'Just as I thought,' said the king. 'Well, I don't want any of those things. I want a SURPRISE!'

The people said nothing.

'Who can give me a surprise?' asked the king.

At last a man answered. 'Your Majesty, whenever we think of a surprise, you want to know what it is and, because you are the king, we have to tell you ... so ... it isn't a surprise any more.'

The king looked very sulky. 'Just as I thought,' he grumbled. 'Well, if I can't have a surprise on my birthday, and you won't tell me what it is, then I won't have a birthday. And if the king doesn't have a birthday, neither shall anyone else. There'll be no more birthdays in the Kingdom of Oldendays until someone gives me a surprise!'

Just then he noticed Sally. 'Who's that?' he said, pointing.

'Please, King Oldendays,' she said when she had reached the king's balcony, 'I come from Nowadays.'

'And what have you got in your hand?' asked the king.

'My magic rattle,' answered Sally.

'A magic rattle!' said the king. 'Why is it magic? What does it do?'

'Well,' said Sally, 'you have to close your eyes . . .' (the king closed his eyes) '. . . and shake the rattle.' The king shook the rattle though Sally held on to it . . . and then . . . oh my goodness, what a surprise when they opened their eyes. For they were no longer standing on a castle balcony overlooking a courtyard, but on the balcony of the block of flats where Sally lived, overlooking a motorway!

'Good gracious!' said the astonished king. 'Where are we?'

'This is Nowadays,' said Sally. 'This is where I live.'

'My word!' said the king, gazing up to the top of the block and then down. 'Nowadays Castle! You must be a very important little girl to live in such a place.'

'I'll be blowed!' he said when he saw the cars driving along, for in Oldendays there weren't any cars.

'Bless my soul!' he said when an aeroplane flew over, for in Oldendays there weren't any aeroplanes.

'Well I AM surprised! And as I've had my

birthday surprise – I think I'd better get back home and tell everybody that they *can* have birthdays after all.'

Sally wasn't quite sure how to get the king back home but she did the only thing possible – closed her eyes and shook the magic rattle, keeping hold of the king's hand ... but his hand slipped slowly away.

'Time for the party, Sally,' called her mother from the hallway.

Sally scrambled out of the bedroom cupboard. If only she could have shown King Oldendays to her mother and baby Tim. Wouldn't *they* have been surprised.

Grandad Gilbert and the special car

Beryl Desmond

Grandad Gilbert worked hard in his garage. There were always cars waiting to be repaired. His grandson Ben loved to help him whenever he could. He was at the garage on the day the important visitor arrived.

'Whoever is this?' Ben called as the big black car drove into Grandad Gilbert's garage.

A tall man wearing a very good suit got out.

'Good morning, sir,' Grandad said, wishing he'd put on his clean overalls.

'Hello, I'd like my car re-sprayed blue,

please,' said the man. 'Could you have it finished by Saturday?'

Grandad looked a little worried. 'The garage is crowded with cars waiting to be repaired,' he told him, 'but I'll do my best.'

Later he drove the car on to the grass beside the garage. 'I'll have to work on it here, my workshop is full,' he decided.

'What's a re-spray, Grandad?' asked Ben.

'It's a new coat of paint that I'll spray on to the car,' said Grandad.

During the next few sunny days he worked hard getting the car prepared. On Friday it was ready. 'The weather's just right,' Grandad told Ben, 'dry but not too hot.'

It was exciting to see the car changing colour as he carefully sprayed on the paint. 'I like the blue colour', said Ben looking at the car.

'Now, it must be left to dry properly,' Grandad said.

They were just enjoying their drinks when . . . 'Oom-pah, oom-pah, boompitty boom.'

'Hurrah, it's a circus parade,' shouted Ben.

Sure enough, a band was leading a procession of caravans, cages and vans along the road. Suddenly, one of the vans pulled into the garage and out tumbled two colourful clowns.

'Hello, can you help us? We've a rattle in our

engine,' they sang, turning three somersaults in the air.

Ben clapped happily.

'I'll take a look,' said Grandad Gilbert.

While he worked, the funny clowns showed Ben how to walk upside down on his hands.

'That's fixed it,' called Grandad. Then he looked up at the sky and saw a black cloud.

Ben saw it too.

'It's going to rain. The re-sprayed car will get wet,' he cried.

Grandad nodded. 'There's no room for it in the garage. It will be spoilt.'

'Leave it to us,' said the clowns, and they got a blue and red bundle from the van. Then they put some poles into the ground.

'I know – they are putting up a circus tent over the car,' shouted Ben excitedly.

Grandad was smiling.

'That's the quickest circus act I've ever seen,' he laughed, as they all ran into the garage, out of the rain.

Meanwhile, underneath the circus tent the newly painted car stayed nice and dry.

Mr Antonio's good turn

David Willmott

It was getting near to the end of January – the time when Mr Antonio the ice-cream man had his holiday. Did you know that ice-cream men have their holidays in the winter when it's cold and nobody wants any ice cream?

When Mr Antonio got up he didn't make any ice cream. Instead he washed up very thoroughly all the pots and pans and spoons and mixing bowls, and made sure that they were spotlessly clean to put away for the winter.

Then he went outside to where he kept his

tricycle and he made sure that was clean too. Then he pumped up the tyres on the tricycle and covered it up for the winter.

'Today,' thought Mr Antonio, 'I can sit by the fire. Then tomorrow I will paint my house.'

As Mr Antonio sat by the fire he thought about all the things that had happened to him during the summer, about all the times he had ridden his tricycle along the straight road with the tall trees, up the long hill, down the other side and over the bridge to the village where all the children lived. He thought of all the times he had rung his bell, and shouted, 'Ice-a-creama, ice-a-creama.'

Mr Antonio was so comfortable that I *think* he dozed off by the fire. He was woken by a loud knocking on his front door, and he heard a lady's voice calling: 'Mr Antonio . . . Mr Antonio.'

Mr Antonio jumped to his feet, put his slippers on and went to the door. 'All right, all right – I'm a-coming,' he said.

When he opened his big front door there was a lady standing there looking very worried. Mr Antonio recognized her as one of the mothers from the village.

'Oh, Mr Antonio,' she said, 'I'm so glad you're here. I think you know my small son, Simon.'

'Oh yes, Simon,' said Mr Antonio. 'He always has an ice-a-creama.'

'That's right,' said Simon's mother. 'Well, you see, it's his birthday today, and the baker's not well and couldn't bake him a cake, and all Simon's friends are coming to tea, and he'll be so disappointed if there's no cake. I wonder, could you please make him an ice-cream cake?'

'Ice-a-creama cake?' said Mr Antonio, wiggling his moustache. 'Now what flavour do you want? I gotta strawberry and vanilla, and chocolate and pistachio – that's the one with the nuts in.'

Simon's mother thought for a moment, then she said, 'I seem to remember that *trifle* ice cream is his favourite.'

'Oh yes, trifle ice-a-creama,' said Mr Antonio, 'I remember we had it when my tricycle fell over. OK you leave it to me.'

So Mr Antonio got out all his pots and pans and spoons, and mixing bowls, and made ice cream as fast as he could. He made all the different flavours – strawberry, vanilla, chocolate, and pistachio. Then he mixed them all together into trifle ice cream which he made into the shape of a cake. Finally, in his best writing he spelt S I M O N on top.

When it was finished Mr Antonio got out his tricycle and put the ice-cream cake very carefully inside. Then he cycled as fast as he could along the road with the tall trees, up the hill, down the other side and over the bridge to the village where the children live.

It was only when he got to Simon's house that he rang his bell and called out, 'Ice-a-creama, ice-a-creama.'

Simon's mother came out of the house and took the cake. 'Thank you very much, Mr Antonio. Come and join the party.'

They gave Mr Antonio a funny hat and a glass of lemonade, and Simon said it was the best birthday he'd ever had.

'Three cheers for Mr Antonio,' said Simon.

'And three cheers for ice-a-creama,' said Mr Antonio.

The fierce lion

Ann Ross

There was once a lion who was very, very fierce. He frightened all the other animals.

One day when the lion was walking through the jungle, he met the chimpanzee who was sitting on the branch of a tree.

'*ROAR*,' said the lion. And the chimp got such a fright, he slipped and fell backwards, and clung on to the branch upside-down with his feet.

'Graw, haw, haw!' laughed the lion,' and he walked on, looking for more mischief.

He came upon a snake who was happily sliding through the grass.

'ROAR!' said the lion. And the snake stopped, poked out her tongue, and slithered up the leg of a nearby giraffe. The giraffe bent his long neck to see what it was. 'Oh, a snake!' he said.

'S-s-sorry about this-s-s,' hissed the snake, 'but Lion gave me such a fright – s-s-s.'

'Graw, haw, haw!' laughed the lion, and he walked on.

Then he came to a river where an elephant was having a drink.

'ROAR!' said the lion. And the elephant was so nervous she lifted her trunk in the air, and squirted water everywhere. Then she ran off, her great ears flapping.

'Graw, haw, haw!' laughed the lion. But this time, he shook with laughter so much that he trod on a sharp little stone. And it got stuck in his paw.

The lion tried to pull it out with his teeth. But the more he tugged and tugged, the deeper the stone went into the soft pad of his paw.

'What shall I do?' wailed the lion. And he called out: 'Help! Help!'

But the other animals stayed hidden: they were too afraid to help the lion because of his fierceness.

The stone became very painful, so the Lion burst out crying!

Just then, a little bird came fluttering through the air.

'Why are you crying, fierce lion?' she asked.

'I have a stone stuck in my paw,' sniffed the lion.

'Poor Lion,' chirped the little bird. 'Perhaps I can help you!' And she flew down next to the lion. She saw his soft pad, and she saw the stone that was stuck in it. *And* she saw the lion's sharp claws! But the bird stuck her little beak into the lion's paw, gripped the stone, and gave a tug.

'Ah!' said the lion. 'It's out! Thank you, little bird.'

The little bird spread out her wings ready to fly off. But then she looked into the lion's eyes. They were friendly! So she closed her wings and stayed where she was, by the lion's paw.

'I don't want to be fierce any more,' said the lion. 'I want to be friendly!'

The little bird flew up into the air, fluttering her wings, calling: 'Lion wants to be friendly!' And all the animals came out of hiding.

The chimp, who was still upside-down in the tree, swung himself right side up. The snake slithered down the giraffe's leg. The elephant came back, trumpeting and running. And all the animals were happy because the lion was never fierce ever again.

Grandma and Bopper Ball go to the seaside

Janet Sorensen

The big rubber ball which Grandma called Bopper Ball was her best friend. A friend who was orangy red in colour, very round, with two wiggly ears to hold on to. A friend who gave Grandma rides on his back.

As Grandma lived by herself, Bopper Ball heard all her news, and went everywhere with her.

One day Grandma decided to go to the seaside. There was a coach that went, and a train, but Grandma didn't go on them. No, *she* would go on Bopper Ball. So she told him her idea. Bopper was delighted. 'Bounce . . . whee . . . bounce,' he said.

Grandma got her old shopping bag and filled it with her sandwiches, a straw hat, a towel and her purse. She tucked her umbrella over her arm, for the *sun* if it was too hot, for *rain* if it was wet. She collected Bopper Ball from the chair in the corner and took him out. She locked the door and straightened her hat.

'It's a lovely sunny morning,' she said, 'and it's *very* early so there won't be many people about. Off we go.'

With her bag on one arm and her umbrella on the other she sat on Bopper Ball and they began to bounce down the path.

Bounce . . . bounce . . . bounce, went Bopper. He usually needed a few bounces before he could begin to bounce into the sky, but this morning he was so excited he bounced over the gate and straight up into the air – high above everything.

'Whee! Whee! We're off to the sea,' shouted Grandma.

Grandma and Bopper bounced along in and out of the clouds . . . too high to be seen from down below . . . only the birds were flying along and they'd seen them before.

Suddenly Grandma shouted, 'Down, Bopper.

I can smell the sea.' And sure enough there was the beach and the sea.

Down, down, they went ... and landed, bounce, on a soft patch of sand.

People were just arriving for a day on the beach. Grandma took off her shoes and stockings and took Bopper to the water. Grandma paddled. 'Ooh! Oooh! Lovely,' she squealed. And Bopper Ball floated gently beside her. The children came to see him.

Bopper liked it by the sea. Grandma took him to sit down. It was getting very hot and Bopper was getting redder and redder. Grandma took the sun hat out of the shopping bag and put it on him. It squashed his ears a bit, but he felt very smart and much cooler. He liked that.

Grandma closed her eyes. 'Just for forty winks.'

Peeping from under his hat, Bopper Ball saw a tiny crab crawling towards him. The crab gave the Bopper Ball a nip. But Bopper was too hard to eat, so the crab crawled away.

Grandma woke up. 'I think I'd like a boat trip,' she said. So they went down the beach and joined the queue for a boat ride.

The boat-man said there was no room for Bopper Ball, so Grandma tied a string to Bopper's ears and trailed him through the water behind the boat. He bobbed up and down. He liked that . . . the water tickled his back and the sun warmed his tummy.

Soon the day was over and Grandma and Bopper Ball, tired but happy, were bouncing into the air for the journey home. Bounce . . . bounce . . . bounce . . . whee.

I wonder if you ever see them . . . keep looking, won't you?

Town Mouse and Country Mouse

Aidan Chambers

There was a Country Mouse who lived a happy life. Her home was in a cosy hole under a hedge, with a field on one side and a little stream trickling by on the other.

One day Country Mouse was visited by Town Mouse. Town Mouse wanted to know all about Country Mouse's life. So Country Mouse took Town Mouse for a walk through her field, and along her stream, and then gave Town Mouse the very best meal she could. There were nuts from the trees and grains of wheat from the field and clear water from the stream.

Afterwards, Town Mouse said, 'Is that all?' She had forgotten her manners because she was so hungry after her walk.

'I'm afraid so,' Country Mouse said. 'I wasn't expecting visitors, you see, and I live very simply.'

'Yes,' Town Mouse said, 'you do. Nothing much seems to happen here. Your life must be very dull. Where I live, I have all sorts of adventures, and there's some terrific food. Maybe you should come back to town with me.'

'It does sound very exciting.'

So that night Country Mouse went to the house where Town Mouse lived. The house was huge, with enormous rooms full of furniture as big as mountains. There were strange machines that hummed and rattled and ticked and glowed.

Town Mouse took Country Mouse to the kitchen. 'This is where I live,' she said, as she gathered a mouth-watering meal. There were five kinds of cheese, thick pieces of beautiful beef fat, crumbly chunks of brown bread, and crunchy bits of icing from a cake.

'You were right,' Country Mouse said, licking her lips and rubbing her paws. 'My life has been much too dull.' And she was just opening her mouth to take a bite of cheese when the kitchen door burst open and in bounded a hairy monster ... that dived straight for Country Mouse, barking and snapping with slavery jaws.

Country Mouse leapt for her life and escaped behind a cupboard in the nick of time.

Town Mouse was already there. 'Dog,' she said, smiling. 'He'll go in a minute. He's got no patience.'

And soon Dog did go, growling with disappointment. 'Come on,' Town Mouse said. 'All clear.'

Fearfully, Country Mouse crept back to her meal. She wasn't feeling quite so hungry now, but she took up a juicy piece of beef fat and was opening her mouth to put it in when she heard a noise that made her shake with terror.

'Me-owww.'

Cat had been waiting silently all the time just outside the kitchen door. Now she pounced, paws flashing and teeth gleaming.

Country Mouse dodged, and ran for her life behind the cupboard again.

Town Mouse was already there. 'A narrow squeak,' she said, grinning. 'We'll be all right here till the morning, then Cat will go away for a sleep.' But Country Mouse, hungry and trembling, didn't close her eyes all night.

When Cat had gone, Town Mouse said, 'The food's still there. We could rush out and grab some, if you like.'

But before Country Mouse could reply, two huge feet came stomping into the room.

'What's this mess!' the feet said. 'Mice again!'

There was a clatter, and a sweeping noise, and when Country Mouse dared look again the food was gone, but the feet were still there. 'I'll put a trap down tonight,' the feet said, and stomped away.

'A trap!' Town Mouse said. 'And Cat as well! We'll have to be really careful tonight.'

Country Mouse sighed. 'You do live in a big and beautiful house,' she said to Town Mouse. 'And there's lots of lovely food. And you do have exciting adventures. But I'm hungry and thirsty and frightened. And I think, after all, if you don't mind, I like my cosy hole under the hedge best because there I can eat and drink when I want to and don't live in fear of cats and dogs and traps and smelly, ugly feet.'

And so Country Mouse said goodbye to Town Mouse and went back to her home under the hedge between the field and the trickling stream.

The crocodile with snappy jaws

Ann Ross

Once, there was a naughty crocodile. He had a long body with scaly skin, a strong swishy, swashy tail, and large snippy, snappy jaws.

He opened his mouth and snapped his jaws not only when he was hungry and having his dinner, but also *between* meals, when he wasn't hungry. He just liked to snap his jaws all day long to frighten the other animals.

Now the larger animals weren't afraid of Crocodile, but they were fed up with the sound of snapping all day.

Rhinoceros said to Crocodile, 'You creaky, snippy, snappy Croc, why don't you keep your jaws shut for a while!'

'No,' snapped Crocodile, 'I like snapping my jaws!' And he dived into the river, splashing Rhinoceros as he went with his swishy, swashy tail.

'Grrrrrr!' said Rhinoceros.

Just then, because Crocodile had jumped into the water and it was safe, Zebra came by to have a drink.

'You look cross,' said Zebra.

'Grrr,' replied Rhinoceros. 'It's Crocodile – he's snapping his jaws again. We must STOP him!'

'I wish we could,' sighed Zebra. 'Because when I come to have a drink, I'm always so frightened he's going to eat me up.'

'Aah, Zebra!' cried Rhinoceros. 'I know what we can do!' And he whispered into Zebra's ear for a long time. Zebra laughed and nodded agreement.

Then Rhinoceros walked over to a tree. He charged at it with his heavy body, and made a branch crash to the ground. He picked the branch up in his huge mouth, and kept it there.

When Crocodile came swimming by and saw

Zebra, he climbed back on to land again, and started snapping his jaws.

But Zebra *didn't* run away.

Crocodile was very surprised. Especially when Zebra said, 'Would you like to eat me up?'

'Oh! But it's not my dinner-time yet,' said Crocodile. 'Still, I can always do with a tasty meal.'

'There is a favour I would like to ask of you first,' said Zebra.

Crocodile swished his tail: 'Well, what is it?'

'Would you please eat me up in one go,' replied Zebra. 'Because I don't want to be eaten up in bits!'

'Oh, I'll eat you any way you want me to,' said Crocodile, and his mouth began to water.

'But to eat me in one go,' said Zebra, 'you will have to open your jaws very, very wide – to fit me in!'

'All right,' said Crocodile. 'I'm ready!'

Crocodile opened his jaws very, *very* wide. And suddenly, just as he was about to snap up Zebra, Rhinoceros threw the branch from his mouth into the air – and it landed right between Crocodile's jaws, just as he closed them in a snap.

'GLUG,' said Crocodile. And he lashed his strong swishy, swashy tail to and fro in anger.

Then Rhinoceros said, 'You creaky Croc, do you promise to stop snapping your jaws between meals?'

'Ges, gi goo,' said Crocodile.

And Rhinoceros *tickled* Crocodile under the chin with his horn, and the branch fell out from his jaws. And Crocodile never snapped ever again, except at dinner-time.

The Trimble Town Band

Beryl Desmond

One day somebody in Trimble Town decided they ought to have a town band. 'A lot of people here play musical instruments,' agreed the townsfolk, so a meeting was arranged for Wednesday evening.

By seven o'clock lots of people were arriving, carrying funny-shaped musical instrument cases.

'I didn't know Mr Ham the butcher played the bassoon,' said Dr Dibble, taking out his trumpet.

Then Mr Toast the baker strolled in carrying his trombone, followed by farmer Crop, struggling through the door with his bass drum.

'Splendid,' cried the chemist, polishing his French horn, 'we've got enough instruments to form a very good band.'

Mrs Read, the librarian, started giving out music. 'I found this march music at the library,' she explained.

Soon they were all ready. 'Right,' shouted someone, 'one ... two ... three ... er ... GO.'

The music began.

Now, the trumpets knew this tune and played it very quickly, 'Parpitty ... parpitty ... parp ... parp ...' However, the trombones had forgotten it and so played very slowly indeed. The tubas didn't know it at all, and soon got lost altogether.

'BOOM, BOOM,' banged farmer Crop happily on his drum. He even added a few extra 'BOOM, BOOMs' just for fun.

'STOP,' shouted Dr Dibble at last, 'STOP.'

Everyone stopped.

'It's awful. We're all playing at different speeds,' he complained.

'We know this march, just follow us,' ordered the trumpets.

'We need to practise. Could you slow down please?' said the trombones.

'Let's play it faster,' shouted farmer Crop, happily.

'We don't know this music. Let's play something else,' grumbled the tubas.

Soon everyone in the hall was arguing loudly. They made so much noise that PC Button, the policeman, heard them. He was on duty outside.

'Now then,' he shouted, entering the hall, 'what's all this?'

'Good evening, Officer,' began Dr Dibble. 'We're arguing about the music.'

PC Button grinned. 'You should listen to your band leader,' he said. 'Who's your leader?'

They looked surprised. 'We ... er ... we haven't got one,' they admitted.

'You must have a band leader to conduct you,' laughed PC Button looking at the music.

Then, to everyone's amazement he held up his hand.

'Let's try the march again at this speed. Not too fast, and not too slow. Watch me and we'll keep together. One, two, three, four.'

The band began to play again. PC Button conducted them very well.

'What a difference a conductor makes,' they all agreed at the end. 'Please will you be our band leader, PC Button?'

PC Button was very honoured.

'I'd love to be,' he replied. 'I'm sure the Trimble Town Band is going to be a very fine band indeed.'

Mrs Tippet's busy day

Valerie McCarthy

Old Mrs Tippet lived with her parrot Nelson, who copied things she said. He could say, 'Good morning', 'Thank you, postman', and 'Two pints, please'. And sometimes even, 'Silly parrot'! He was always picking up things to say.

One morning Mrs Tippet woke up and knew that she was going to be busy that day – but she couldn't remember why.

She went downstairs and made herself some tea and said 'Good morning' to Nelson, who said 'Two pints please' back.

'Silly Parrot,' said Mrs Tippet, smiling, and then she sat down and tried to remember why she was going to be busy.

Just then there was a knock on the door, 'Rat a tat tat'.

It was Mrs Down-the-Road, from round-the-corner.

'Oh dear,' thought Mrs Tippet, 'I haven't got time to see anyone today, because I'm too busy.' But before she had time to tell Mrs Down-the-Road, Nelson called out, 'Come in. Come in and have some tea.'

'Thank you very much, Mrs Tippet, I will,' said Mrs Down-the-Road. And she did!

Mrs Tippet was just about to explain that she was too busy, when the door-knocker went again, 'Rat a tat tat'. It was Mr Stamp the postman. Before Mrs Tippet could speak, Nelson called, 'Come in. Come in and have some tea.'

'Don't mind if I do,' said Mr Stamp. And he did.

'Oh dear, oh dear,' thought Mrs Tippet, and then the door knocker sounded again, 'Rat a tat tat'. It was Miss Peardrop from the sweetshop. Mrs Tippet opened her mouth but Nelson called out, 'Come in. Come in and have some tea.'

'How kind – I'd love to,' said Mrs Peardrop. And she did.

Mrs Tippet sighed and put the kettle on, and

then there was another knock on the door, 'Rat a tat tat'.

This time it was Mr Crust the baker, holding a big box tied with ribbon. Nelson called out, 'Come in. Come in and have some tea.'

'I certainly will,' said Mr Crust. And he handed Mrs Tippet the box. 'Here's your birthday cake, just like you ordered,' he said.

Then Mrs Tippet remembered. Today was her birthday. She *was* going to be busy – having a party. And here she was, already having it!

She made the tea and cut the cake, giving everybody a big slice. And then she cut an extra big slice for Nelson. When she gave it to him, he said, 'Silly parrot!' But she could have sworn that he was winking at her!

Bopper Ball goes out alone

Janet Sorensen

Grandma's best friend Bopper Ball liked living with Grandma and loved all the bouncy rides he took her for . . . sometimes bouncing along the paths . . . sometimes high into the air – up in the sky, above everything.

Bopper was a very special large magic ball, very round and orangey-red in colour, with two ears to hold on to when Grandma rode along.

One day when Grandma locked the doors and windows and went to bed she forgot to put Bopper Ball in the shed where he lived. She left him out in the back yard. Bopper was very cross. He felt cold and started to bounce to get warm.

Bounce . . . bounce . . . bounce, he went, and suddenly he gave an extra high bounce . . . went right over the fence . . . and found he was out in the street.

'Mmmmm,' said Bopper. He thought how nice it was out on the street on his own, and decided to go for a bounce around.

He set off, keeping to the paths. All the curtains were closed – everyone had gone to bed – only the moon watched him.

Suddenly Bopper Ball, bouncing along happily, bounced into a black and white striped pole.

'What do you think you are doing, you big red ball with ears?' said a voice. 'I'm a *nice* orange ball. I'm a beacon and I show people where to cross the road. I go on and off and I guard the zebra crossing.'

Bopper Ball bounced round and round, he couldn't see a zebra crossing anything. Funny chap, thought Bopper as he bounced on.

Then he came to some traffic lights. Bopper looked at them . . . red . . . yellow . . . green. He wished they wouldn't keep blinking on and off and changing.

'Red means stop,' said the red traffic light.
'Yellow means get ready,' said yellow.

'And I say go,' said the green light.

There are some funny things at the top of poles, thought Bopper – and went on his bouncing way.

The next pole Bopper saw had a circle at the top with 'three-o' in big black letters.

That means 'thirty', thought Bopper. That means how fast the cars can go. And he bounced along very fast.

Hope I'm not going too fast, he thought.

The next pole Bopper saw had a blue circle with white arrows going round. A roundabout sign . . . and in the light of the moon, Bopper danced round and round on the grass in the middle of the roundabout. Bounce . . . bounce . . . bounce.

Before crossing the road Bopper bounced carefully, looking both ways. Then he bounced across. After that he rested on the edge of the pavement.

'You mustn't stop here,' said a loud voice. 'I'm a yellow line. Cars can't stop here, and neither can you.'

'You mustn't stop here,' 'You mustn't stop here,' said two voices together, which were double yellow lines. 'Move on, move on.'

Bopper Ball was tired and moved on slowly. Bounce . . . . . . bounce . . . . . . bounce. He moved more and more slowly. . . .

'I know you, don't I?' said a voice behind him. And there was a policeman. 'I know where you live. A Bopper like you should be at home in bed. Mind if I *ride* you home?'

So if you *had* looked out of your window last night you might have seen a policeman bouncing along the road on a bopper.

'Not a word to anyone, eh!' said the policeman, as he put Bopper over the fence into Grandma's garden.

'No,' said Bopper. He was very tired, but what a lot he'd seen. What a shame Grandma wasn't there too, he thought – and then fell asleep.

Acknowledgements

'Monty the Monkey' was first published as 'Monty's Muddled Monday' in *The Rainbow Storybook* (Methuen, 1981).
'Fox Tricks' by Aidan Chambers is adapted from 'Fox and Goat' and 'Fox and Cock' from *Fox Tricks* (Heinemann, 1981).